First Science Dictionary

Jean M. Shaw
Richard W. Dyches

Illustrated by Czeslaw Sornat

Franklin Watts

New York • London • Toronto • Sydney

The authors wish to thank the following people for their assistance
in evaluating this manuscript.

Iva D. Brown, Ed. D.
Department of Science Education
University of Southern Mississippi
Hattiesburg, Mississippi

Marilyn S. Neil, Ph.D.
Associate Professor of Education
Georgia Southwestern College
Americus, Georgia

James D. Cowles, Ph.D.
Department of Early Childhood Education
United States International University
San Diego, California

Patricia M. Wilson, M.A.
Adjunct Professor of Education
Mercy College
Dobbs Ferry, New York

Patsy Ann Giese, Ph.D.
Associate Professor of Educational Studies
Slippery Rock University
Slippery Rock, Pennsylvania

Editorial Development: The Pegasus Group
Design and Production: The Pegasus Group

For Katie and Matt
Jordana, Michael, and Kate

Library of Congress Cataloging-in-Publication Data
Shaw, Jean M.
First science dictionary / by Jean M. Shaw
and Richard W. Dyches.
p.   cm.
Summary: Illustrations and simple definitions explain over
260 science terms.
ISBN 0-531-15237-5   ISBN 0-531-11110-5 (lib. bdg.)
1. Science—Dictionaries, Juvenile.
[1. Science—Dictionaries.]
I. Dyches, Richard W.   II. Title.
Q123.S513   1991
503—dc20
91-7528   CIP   AC

Dear Parent and Educator:

Science should be a subject that encourages children's natural curiousity, yet in their early school years they are often overwhelmed by the terminology and concepts. In the science-oriented world of today it is especially important for children in grades K-3 to develop a strong science vocabulary. The *First Science Dictionary* provides definitions of more than 260 key terms that children must know in order to understand the more complex science concepts they will study in grades 4 and up.

Through the use of this reference book, science becomes a wonderful learning experience. Children read the simple definitions, then see the terms further explained by visual representations, such as a scholarly skunk examining a fossil and other animals experimenting with weight and measure. Science becomes more meaningful when children see it as it relates to a world familar to them.

The *First Science Dictionary* reflects an extensive review of the curriculum and correlates with all major science textbooks. Furthermore, the dictionary follows the curriculum guidelines set by the National Science Teachers Association.

We believe that this subject-focused dictionary and its companion, the *First Math Dictionary,* are unique in that they teach a subject and at the same time encourage good reference skills by introducing children to alphabetized key terms.

We are confident that children who use this important reference tool will learn the science terms and concepts they need both in their classrooms and in their everyday lives.

Sincerely,

Richard W. Dyches

Jean M. Shaw

ABOUT THE AUTHORS

Dr. Richard W. Dyches is a consultant and writer of educational materials for young children. A former elementary teacher and college professor, Dr. Dyches frequently lectures at national and international workshops and conferences. He lives in New York City.

Dr. Jean M. Shaw is a Professor of Elementary and Early Childhood Education at the University of Mississippi. She is a nationally known educator and author of many books for young children in the areas of math and science. Dr. Shaw lives in Oxford, Mississippi.

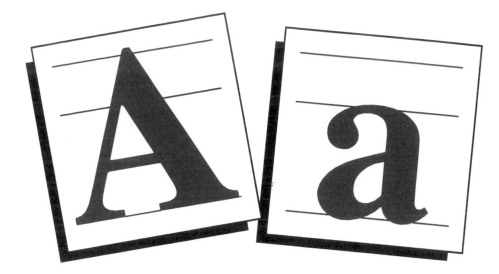

Aa

abdomen

The **abdomen** is between the chest and the legs.

air

Air is the mixture of gases that is all around us.

amphibian

An **amphibian** is an animal that can live on land and in water.

animal

An **animal** is a living thing that eats and moves about on its own.

Aa

ankle

The **ankle** is between the foot and the leg.

aquarium

An **aquarium** is a place where sea creatures are protected and studied.

arm

The **arm** is between the shoulder and the hand.

arrange

When you **arrange** things, you put them in some kind of order.

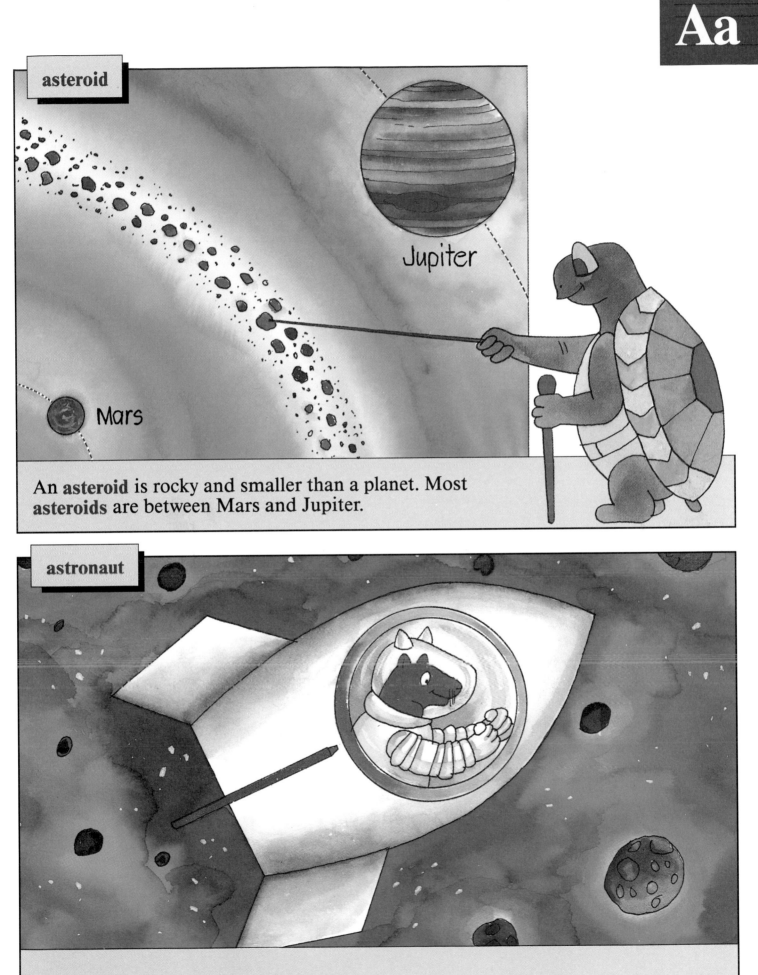

asteroid

Jupiter

Mars

An **asteroid** is rocky and smaller than a planet. Most **asteroids** are between Mars and Jupiter.

astronaut

An **astronaut** is a space traveler.

battery	Big Dipper
A **battery** can store and make electricity.	The **Big Dipper** is a constellation.

Bb

bird

A **bird** is an animal with feathers. Most **birds** fly.

body

head

shoulder

chest

hip

leg

foot

The **body** is the whole makeup of something.

9

Bb

boil

Water **boils** when it gets very hot. Liquids bubble when they **boil**.

bone

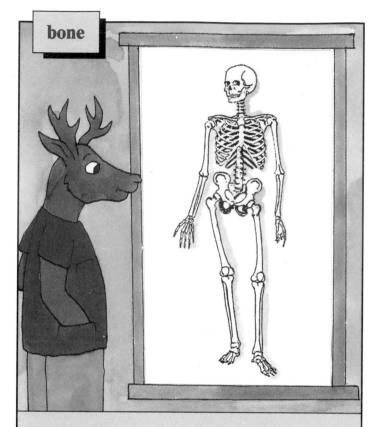

Bones are hard. **Bones** form the skeletons of many animals.

bread

Bread is one kind of food made from grain.

breeze

A **breeze** is a gentle wind.

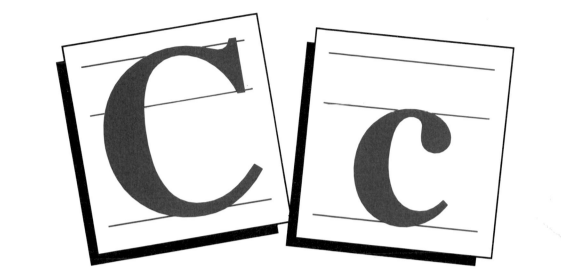

cactus

A **cactus** is a plant that needs little water. It is usually prickly.

capacity

Capacity is how much a container holds.

centimeter

You use **centimeters** to measure length.

cereal

Cereal is one kind of food made from grain.

cereal

cereal

milk

classify

You **classify** things that are similar when you put them in groups.

claw

eagle

duck

tiger

Some animals have **claws** at the ends of their toes.

clean

Clean means free from dirt.

climate

Climate is the usual weather over a long time.

cloud

A **cloud** is made up of tiny drops of water or ice particles.

coast

Land and ocean meet at a **coast**.

cold

When the temperature is low, it is **cold**.

color

Color lets us see the difference among things that are alike.

comet

A **comet** is made of gas, dust, and ice. **Comets** travel around the sun.

communicate

We **communicate** when we give information about things.

compare

SPIDER

BEETLE

When you **compare**, you tell how things are alike and different.

compound machine

A **compound machine** is made of simple machines.

Cc

conclusion

A **conclusion** is an opinion or a decision made after an observation or experience.

conductor

A **conductor** lets electricity, heat, and sound travel. The wire is a **conductor**.

conifer

A **conifer** is a tree with cones.

conservation

Conservation means taking care of nature.

constellation

A **constellation** is a group of stars that seem to have the shape of someone or something.

Cc

crater

A **crater** is a hole shaped like a bowl.

crystal

A **crystal** is a solid that forms in a special shape.

cup

You use a **cup** to measure capacity.

current

A **current** is the flow of water, wind, or electricity.

customary measure

Some **customary measures** are inches, pounds, and cups.

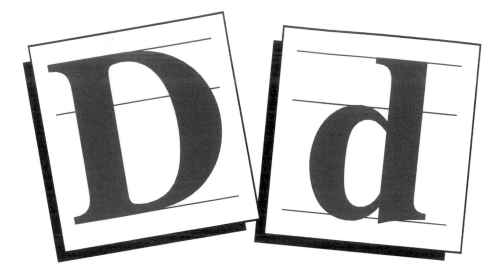

danger

Danger is the possibility of harm.

dark

It is **dark** when there is little or no light.

day

Day is the time between sunrise and sunset. It is light during the **day**.

deciduous

SUMMER   WINTER

Deciduous trees lose their leaves every year.

degree

You measure temperature in **degrees**.

desert

A **desert** gets very little rain.

Dd

Dew is little drops of water that form when the ground cools.

Your **diet** is what you eat.

Different means not the same.

It is hard to see in **dim** light.

dinosaur

Dinosaurs were animals that lived long ago.

Dd

dissolve

When something **dissolves**, it mixes with a liquid and seems to disappear.

drought

A **drought** is when a long time passes without rain.

drug

A **drug** is a substance used in medicine. If **drugs** are abused, they are harmful.

dull

Dull means not sharp or not shiny. The pipe is **dull**.

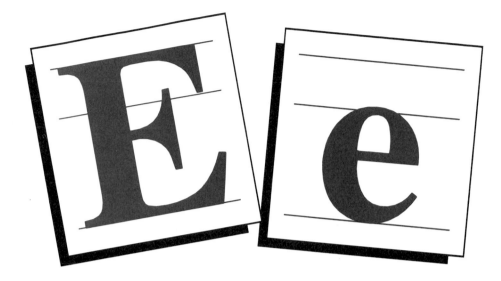

ear

The **ear** is the body part for hearing.

Earth

Earth is the third planet from the sun. People live on **Earth**.

earthquake

An **earthquake** shakes or slides the ground.

earthworm

An **earthworm** lives and moves in the soil.

egg

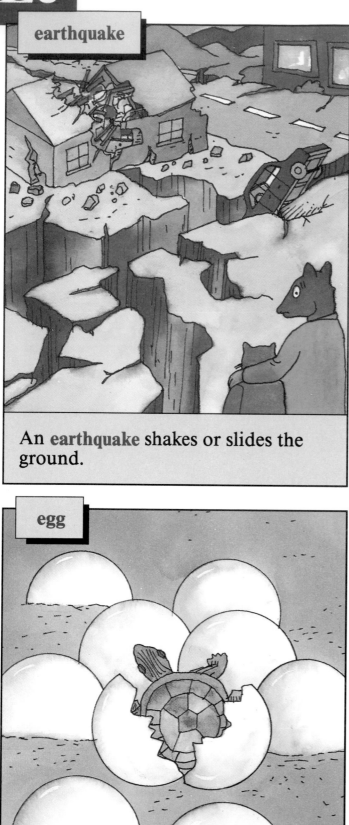

Animals reproduce from **eggs**.

elbow

elbow

The **elbow** is where the arm bends.

electricity

Electricity is energy that can be changed into light, heat, and sound energy.

endangered animal

There is a chance that **endangered animals** will die out unless they are protected.

energy

Energy gives the power for doing work.

erosion

Erosion wears away the earth's surface.

Ee

evaporate

When water **evaporates,** tiny invisible particles go into the air.

exercise

Exercise is activity that helps keep you healthy.

experiment

You can **experiment** to find answers.

eye

The **eye** is the body part for seeing.

fall

Fall is the time of year between summer and winter. **Fall** days are short and cool.

fern

A **fern** is a plant with long feathery leaves and no flowers.

29

feather

Feathers cover a bird's body.

fire

A fire gives off heat and light when fuel burns.

fish

A fish is an animal with gills and fins. Fish live in water.

float

When an object floats, it stays up in air or water.

flood

Too much rain can cause a **flood**.

flower

A **flower** is the part of a plant that helps to make fruit.

fog

Fog is a low cloud.

food chain

A **food chain** shows how the foods eaten by different animals are related.

food groups

Cereal

milk

bread and cereal

meat

fruit and vegetables

Food helps living things grow and stay healthy. There are four **food groups**.

fossil

A **fossil** is a print or a part of a plant or animal. It is hard like stone.

freeze

A liquid **freezes** when it gets very cold and changes to a solid.

fresh water

Fresh water is not salty. Most rivers and lakes contain **fresh water**.

friction

Rubbing surfaces together causes **friction**.

fruit

A **fruit** is part of a plant with seeds inside.

fuel

A **fuel** is something that burns to provide energy.

fungus

Fungus grows from tiny spores. Mold and mushrooms are examples of **fungus**.

gas

A **gas** is a substance that has no size or shape. A **gas** can fill any space.

gear

A **gear** is a wheel with teeth that fit into the teeth of another wheel.

germ

A **germ** is a tiny living thing that might cause disease.

globe

A **globe** is a model of the earth.

gram

You use **grams** to measure mass.

grass

Grass is a plant with narrow leaves.

Gg

gravity

Gravity is the force that pulls things toward Earth.

group

A **group** is a collection or a set of objects or living things.

grow

Grow means to become larger.

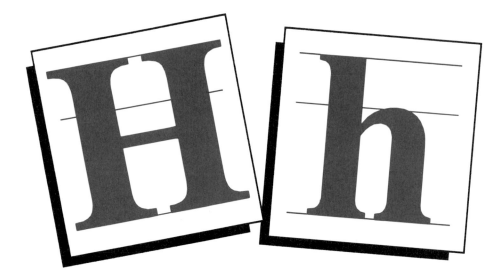

habitat

The place where plants or animals usually live is their **habitat**.

Hh

hair

Hair grows from the skin of mammals.

hand

A **hand** is at the end of an arm. It is used for holding things.

hard

Hard objects are firm.

heat

Heat is energy that makes things feel warm or hot.

hear

Animals use their ears to hear sounds.

heavy

A heavy object is hard to pick up.

High can mean tall or the pitch of a sound.

hurricane

A **hurricane** is a strong storm that forms over the ocean.

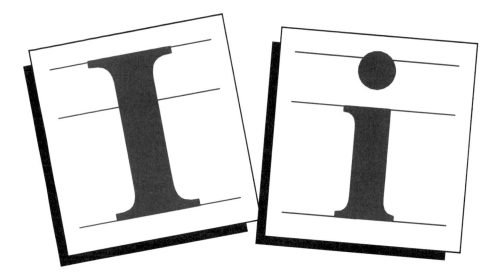

ice

Ice is frozen water.

identify

flower

leaves

stem

roots

When you name things, you **identify** them.

Ii

inclined plane

An **inclined plane** is a simple machine.
A ramp is an **inclined plane**.

inflate

Inflate means to fill with air.

insect

An **insect** is an animal with six legs and three body parts.

instrument

You use **instruments** to measure or record.

insulator

ICE

An **insulator** stops heat, electricity, or sound from traveling well.

investigate

Will it float? Will it sink?

To **investigate** is to use your mind and senses to find out more about things.

island

Land surrounded by water is an **island**.

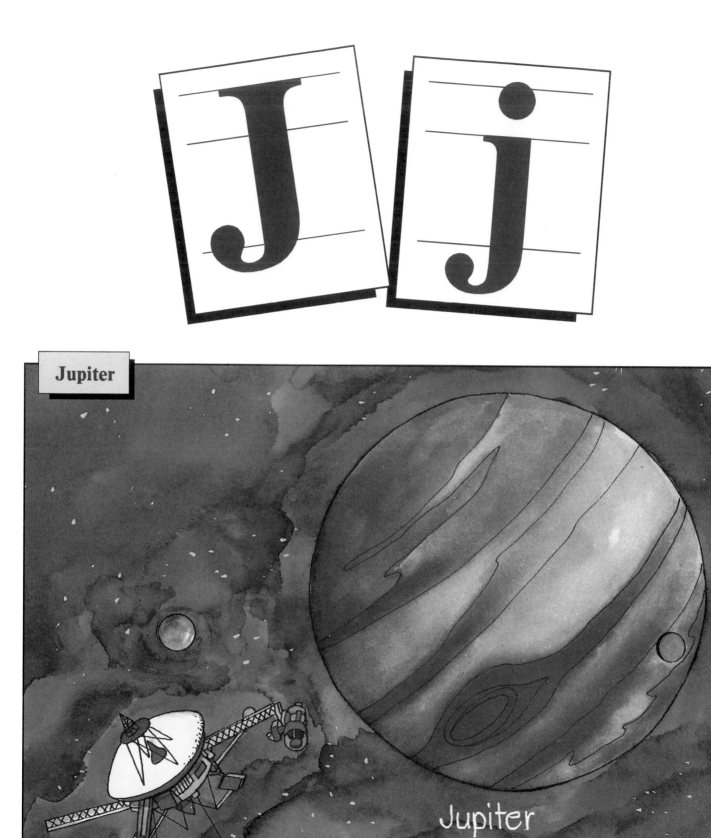

Jupiter

The largest planet in our solar system is **Jupiter**. It is fifth from the sun.

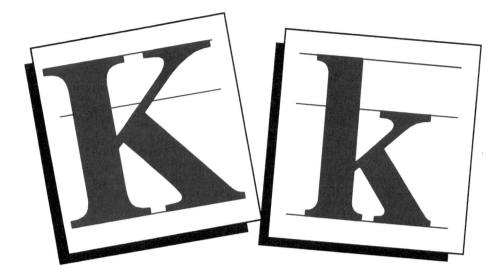

kilogram

You use **kilograms** to measure weight and mass.

laboratory

Some scientists work in a **laboratory**.

lake

A **lake** is a large body of water with land all around it.

leaf

A **leaf** is a flat, green part of a plant. A plant makes food in its **leaves**.

leg

The **leg** is between the hip and the foot.

lens

A **lens** is made of transparent material. Its shape can make things look larger or smaller.

lever

A **lever** is a simple machine that is a long bar or rod.

Ll

lift

You **lift** objects to move them.

light

Light is energy that lets us see.

lightning

Lightning is a flash of light in the sky. It is caused by electricity.

liquid

A **liquid** flows. It takes the shape of its container.

liter

You use **liters** to measure capacity.

living thing

A **living thing** moves, eats, grows, breathes, and can reproduce.

loud

A **loud** sound is very noisy.

low

Low can mean close to the ground or the pitch of a sound.

Machines help do work.

A **magnet** attracts or picks up objects of iron and some other metals.

mammal

A **mammal** is an animal. Mother **mammals** can make their own milk to feed their babies.

Mm

map

A **map** is a drawing or picture that shows important parts of an area.

Mars

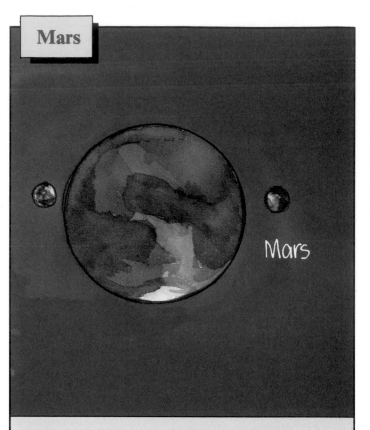

Mars

Mars is the fourth planet from the sun.

mass

Mass is the amount of material in an object.

match

Birds

Trees

Flowers

Objects **match** if they are alike or go together.

measure

You **measure** size, weight, temperature, capacity, and time.

meat

Meat is a food that comes from animals.

melt

When solids **melt**, they become liquid.

Mercury

Mercury

Mercury is the planet closest to the sun.

Mm

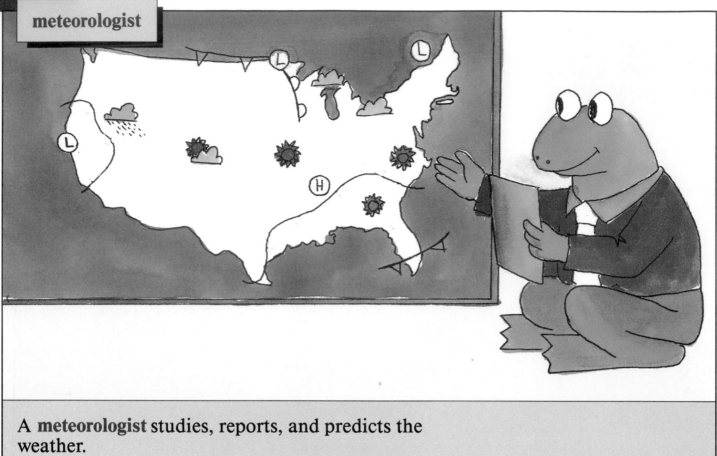

A **meteorologist** studies, reports, and predicts the weather.

meter

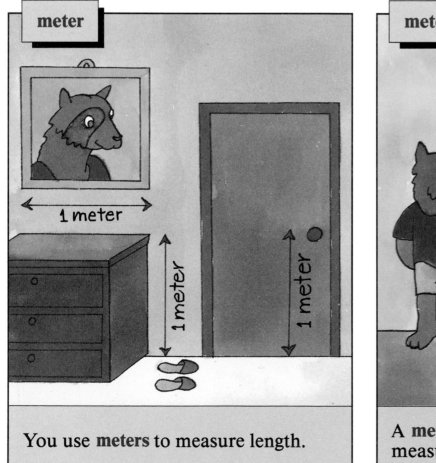

1 meter

1 meter

1 meter

You use **meters** to measure length.

meterstick

A **meterstick** is a tool used to measure length.

54

metric measure

1 L = 1,000 ml
1 m = 100 cm
1 km = 1,000 m
1 kg = 1,000 g

Some **metric measures** are centimeter, square meter, liter, and kilogram.

Mm

microscope

A **microscope** uses lenses to make small objects look larger.

milk

Milk is a food that helps build strong teeth and bones.

milliliter

You use **milliliters** to measure capacity.

mineral

A **mineral** is a substance from the earth's crust. Gold, iron, copper, and salt are **minerals**.

mold

Mold is a fungus that grows best in warm, damp places.

mollusk

A **mollusk** is an animal with a soft body and no bones. Many **mollusks** have shells.

month

A **month** is part of a year. It has 28 to 31 days.

Mm

moon

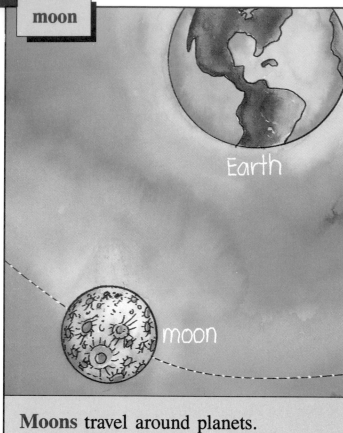

Moons travel around planets. Earth has one **moon**.

moss

Moss is a small, soft plant.

mountain

A **mountain** is a very high part of the earth's crust.

mouth

The **mouth** is the body opening where an animal takes in food.

move

When something **moves**, it changes place or position.

nature

Nature is the out-of-doors world.

neck

The **neck** connects the head and the body.

Neptune

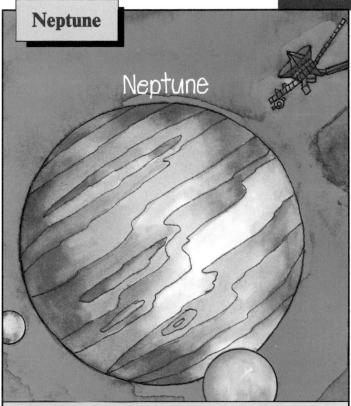

Neptune is a large planet far from the sun. It has many moons.

night

Night is the time between sunset and sunrise. It is dark during the **night**.

nose

The **nose** is the body part for smelling.

observe

To **observe** is to get information by using your senses.

ocean

The **ocean** is salty water covering nearly three fourths of the earth.

Oo

odor

An **odor** is a smell.

opaque

You cannot see through **opaque** materials.

orbit

Earth

Moon

orbit

An **orbit** is a path around an object.

oxygen

Oxygen is a colorless, odorless, tasteless gas found in air and water. Animals need **oxygen** to live.

63

P p

pet

Animals that live with people are called **pets.**

photosynthesis

In **photosynthesis,** plants use air, sunlight, and water to make their own food.

pitch

Pitch is how low or high a sound is.

plane

A flat, level surface is a **plane**.

planet

There are nine **planets** in our solar system. They orbit around the sun.

plant

A **plant** is a living thing that makes its own food.

Pp

plant embryo

embryo

A **plant embryo** is inside a seed and is the beginning of a new plant.

Pluto

Pluto

Pluto is a planet very far from the sun. It has one large moon.

poison

Poison can make you sick or even kill you if you eat or drink it. *Never* eat, drink, or touch **poison**.

pollution

Pollution means dirtying the air, water, or soil with harmful things.

precipitation

Precipitation is rain, snow, hail, or sleet.

predict

You **predict** when you use what you know to guess in advance what will happen.

prism

A **prism** is a transparent object that can break light into a rainbow of colors.

pry

For: Rabbit

Pry means to move or raise something by using a lever.

pull

You **pull** when you move something toward you.

pulley

A **pulley** is a simple machine with a wheel, groove, and rope.

push

You **push** when you move something away from you.

quiet

When there is little noise, it is **quiet**.

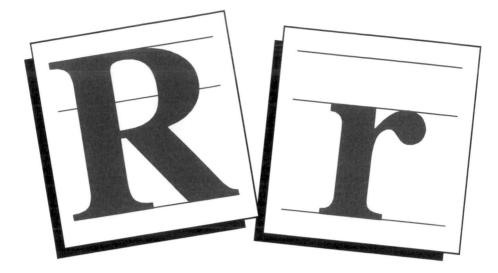

Rr

Rain is drops of water that fall from the clouds.

A **rain gauge** is used to measure the amount of rain.

recycle

You **recycle** when you use materials again.

reflect

When light is **reflected,** it bounces off a surface.

repel

Repel means to push things away. Magnets can **repel** one another.

Rr

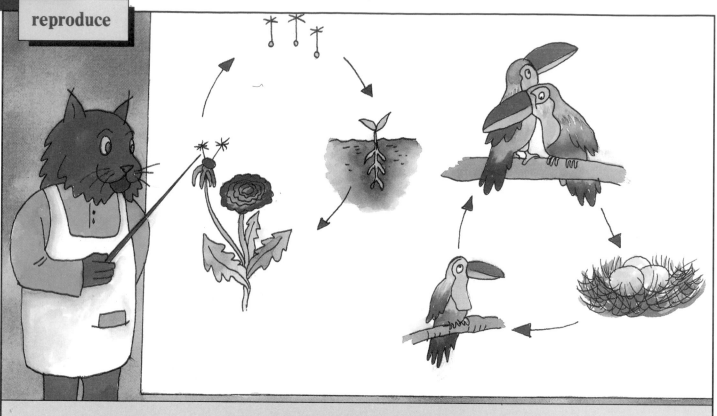

reproduce

Animals and plants **reproduce** when they make new life of their own kind.

reptile

A **reptile** is an animal with dry, scaly skin.

reservoir

A **reservoir** is a lake where water is collected and stored.

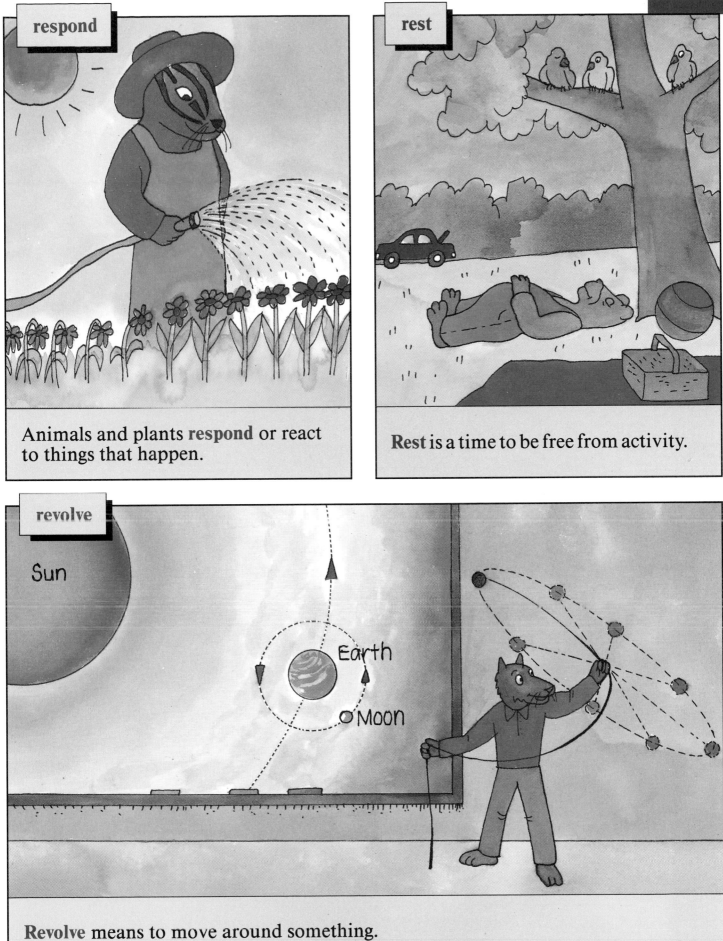

respond

Animals and plants **respond** or react to things that happen.

rest

Rest is a time to be free from activity.

revolve

Sun

Earth

Moon

Revolve means to move around something.

river

A **river** is a large, natural stream of water.

rock

A **rock** is a hard piece of the earth's crust made up of minerals.

roll

To **roll** is to move a round object by turning it over and over.

root

The **root** of a plant stores food and holds the plant in the ground.

ruler

A **ruler** is a tool used to measure length.

Rr

safety

Safety is being careful to prevent accidents and avoid danger.

same

TOY SALE
2 for 1

Things that are the **same** are alike in some way.

sand

Sand is made of tiny pieces of rock.

satellite

A **satellite** travels around a planet.

Saturn

Saturn

Saturn is the sixth planet from the sun. **Saturn** has beautiful rings.

scale

A **scale** is a tool used to measure mass or weight.

science

Science is a process involving people in observing, investigating, experimenting, and forming conclusions.

scientist

A **scientist** observes, investigates, experiments, and forms conclusions.

screw

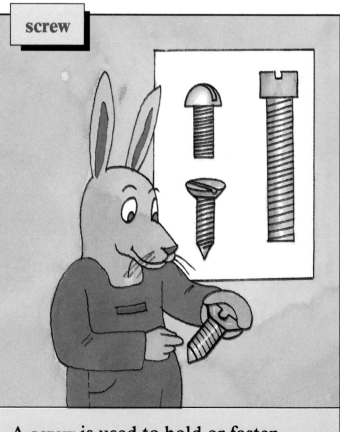

A **screw** is used to hold or fasten things. It has grooves.

sea creature

A **sea creature** is an animal that lives in or near the ocean.

season

Earth's year has four **seasons**—winter, spring, summer, and fall.

seed

A **seed** is the part of a plant that grows into a new plant.

Ss

sense

see

hear

taste

touch   smell

An animal's five **senses** are seeing, hearing, tasting, touching, and smelling.

shadow

When light is blocked by an object, you see a **shadow**.

shell

A **shell** is the hard outer covering of some animals.

shiny

A **shiny** object is bright and gleaming.

shrub

A **shrub** is a woody plant that is smaller than a tree.

simple machine

A **simple machine** helps do work. Levers and pulleys are **simple machines.**

skeleton

A **skeleton** is made up of the bones of an animal.

skin

The **skin** is the soft outer covering of an animal. The **skin** is the body part for touch.

skull

The bones of an animal's head form the **skull**.

slide

Objects **slide** easily on a smooth or slanted surface.

snow

Snow is frozen water. It falls from the clouds as soft white flakes.

soft

Soft things are fluffy or spongy, not hard.

soil

Soil is part of the top layer of the earth's crust. Plants grow in **soil**.

solar system

Sun

Mercury

Venus

Earth

Mars

Jupiter

Saturn

Neptune

Pluto

Uranus

The **solar system** includes the sun and all bodies that revolve around it.

solid

A **solid** has a shape of its own.

sort

green glass   plastic   clear glass   paper

When you **sort**, you put objects in groups.

sound

Sound is something you hear.

spaceship

A **spaceship** is used to travel through space.

space shuttle

A **space shuttle** is used for trips between Earth and space.

space suit

A **space suit** makes working in space possible.

spider

A **spider** is an animal with eight legs and two body parts.

spore

A **spore** is a very tiny part that can grow into mold.

spring

Spring is the time of year between winter and summer. Plants begin to grow in the **spring**.

star

A **star** produces its own light. Many **stars** can be seen in the sky at night.

static electricity

Static electricity makes your hair stand on end when you brush it.

steam

Steam is small drops of water that form above boiling water.

stem

stem →

The **stem** of a plant holds up the flower and leaves.

stomach

stomach

The **stomach** helps an animal break down food.

storm

A **storm** is weather with strong wind, rain, snow, or hail.

summer

Summer is the time of year between spring and fall. **Summer** days are long and warm.

sun

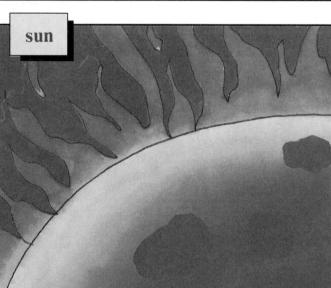

The **sun** is the star in the center of our solar system. It gives off light and heat.

sundial

A **sundial** is a kind of clock. You can tell time by the shadow cast on it.

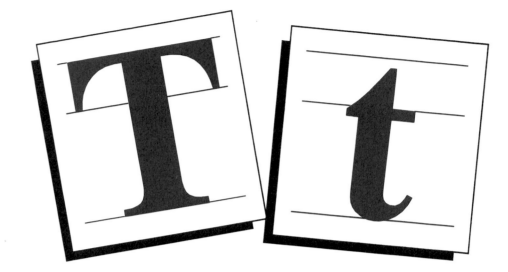

taste

Animals **taste** foods and drinks by eating or drinking them.

Tt

telescope

A **telescope** uses lenses to make faraway objects appear closer.

temperature

Temperature is a measure of how hot or cold something is.

texture

Texture is the way something feels or looks.

thermometer

A **thermometer** is used to measure how hot or cold something is.

Tt

thigh

The **thigh** is part of the leg between the hip and the knee.

thunder

Thunder is the noise that is caused by lightning during a storm.

tongue

An animal's **tongue** is in its mouth. It helps in tasting, eating, and making sounds.

tornado

A **tornado** is a strong storm with whirling winds.

translucent

You see a cloudy picture through **translucent** materials.

transparent

You can see clearly through **transparent** materials.

tree

A **tree** is a large plant with a trunk, branches, and leaves.

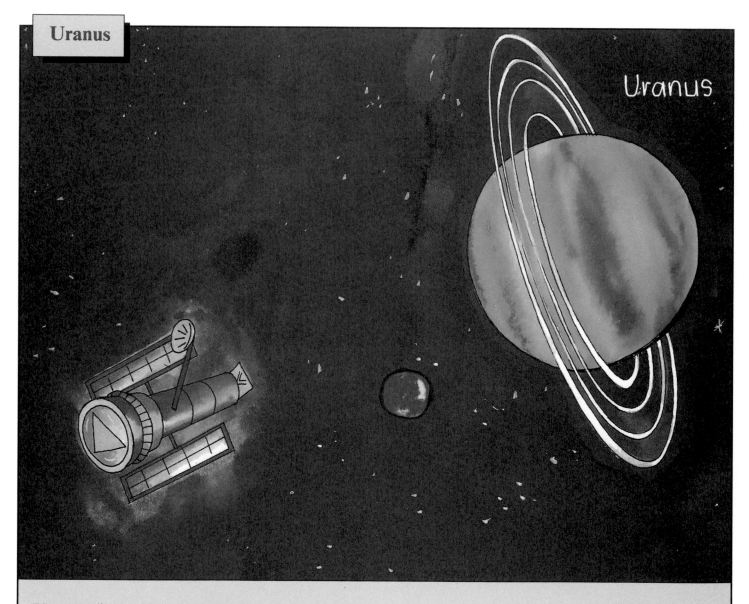

Uranus

Uranus

Uranus is a planet with moons and rings.

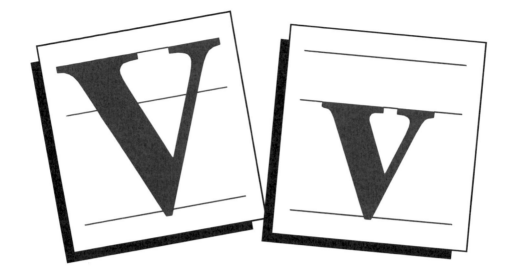

valley

A **valley** is low land between hills or mountains.

vapor

vaporizer

Vapor is tiny drops of water found in steam, clouds, or in the air.

vegetable

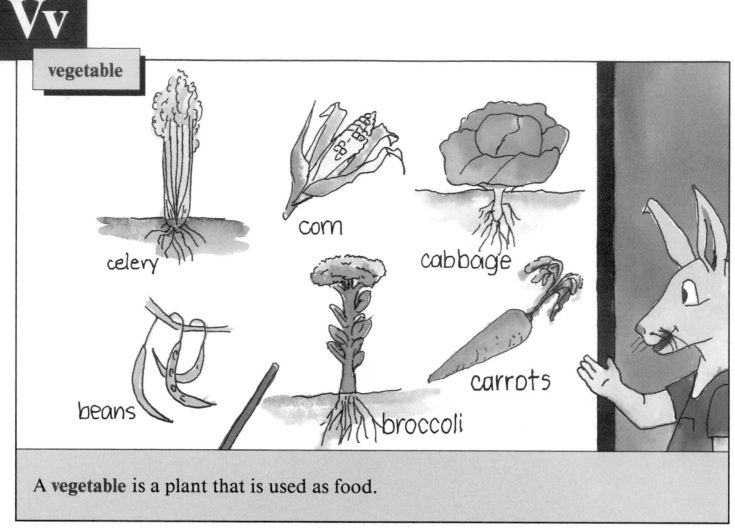

celery

corn

cabbage

beans

broccoli

carrots

A **vegetable** is a plant that is used as food.

vein

A **vein** is like a tube. It carries blood in animals or water in plants.

Venus

Venus

Venus is the second planet from the sun. **Venus** is covered by clouds.

vibration

Vibrations are caused when air or objects move rapidly back and forth.

vine

A **vine** is a plant with a long, winding stem.

volcano

A **volcano** is a hill or mountain that has a crater. When it erupts, hot lava flows out.

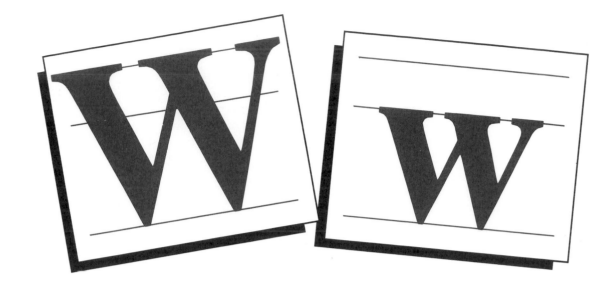

waist

The **waist** is between the ribs and the hips.

water

Water is a tasteless, colorless, odorless liquid. All living things need **water**.

weather

Weather is the condition of the air at a certain time and place.

weather vane

A **weather vane** shows the direction from which the wind is blowing.

wedge

A **wedge** is a simple machine. It is used to pry objects apart.

weed

A **weed** is a plant growing where it is not wanted.

week

Things To Do	
Monday	Clean my room
Tuesday	Play soccer
Wednesday	Go to the movies
Thursday	Wash
Friday	See
Saturday	
Sunday	Picnic

A **week** is seven days.

wheel

A **wheel** is a simple machine. It moves things by rolling.

wind

Wind is moving air. **Winds** may be gentle breezes or part of strong storms.

winter

Winter is the time of year between fall and spring.
Winter days are short.

wire

Wire is a thin metal thread. It can be used to conduct electricity.

work

Work is an effort made to move things.

An **x-ray** is a special picture that shows the inside of something or someone.

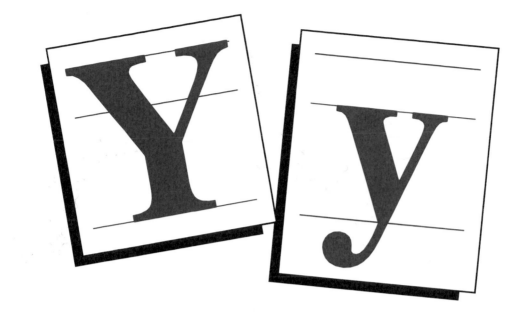

year

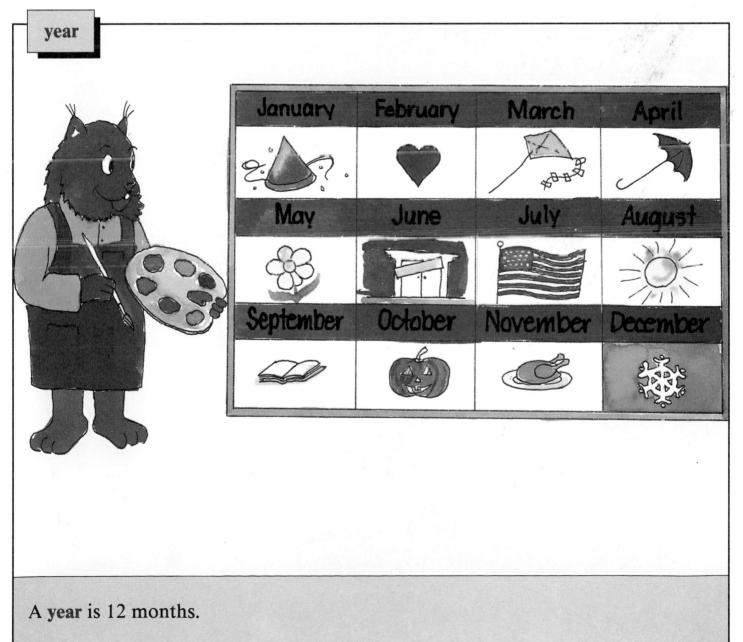

January	February	March	April
May	June	July	August
September	October	November	December

A **year** is 12 months.

A **zoo** is a place where animals are protected and studied.